LAMPS
FROM THE ATHENIAN AGORA

AMERICAN SCHOOL OF CLASSICAL STUDIES AT ATHENS
PRINCETON, NEW JERSEY
1963

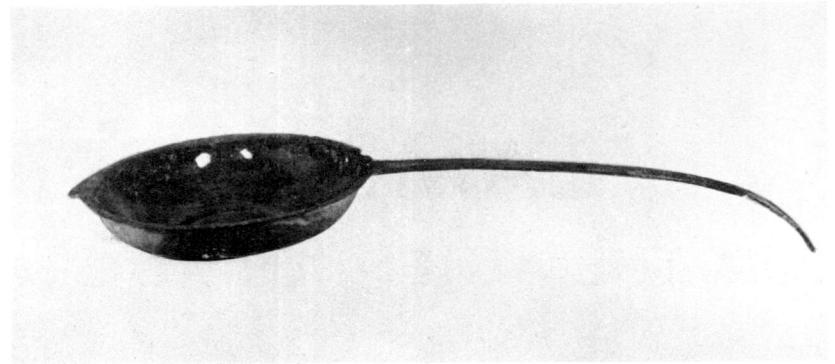

1. Copper Lamp from a Mycenaean Chamber Tomb, about 1450 B.C. B 704.

Pallas Athene went in front with a golden lamp, making a very fine light.

Homer, *Odyssey* XIX

Homer speaks of a lamp this once, when Odysseus and Telemachus working at night to remove the shields and spears out of their enemies' reach have their palace lit up by Athena, herself invisible.

After Mycenaean times the Athenians had no lamps until the early 7th century when the handmade lamp (2) appeared, an idea from the east. The development of the Attic clay lamp from this shape is illustrated on four pages at the end. The shape itself lived on in the east for millennia and reappeared in Attica in the 11th century A.D. (3).

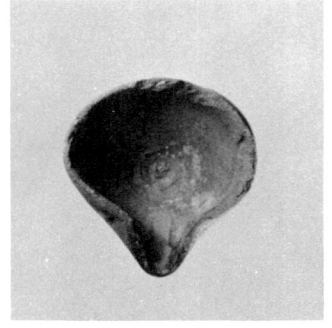

2. 7th century B.C. L 564.   3. 11th century A.D. L 1612.

LAMPS
FROM THE ATHENIAN AGORA

AMERICAN SCHOOL OF CLASSICAL STUDIES AT ATHENS
PRINCETON, NEW JERSEY
1963

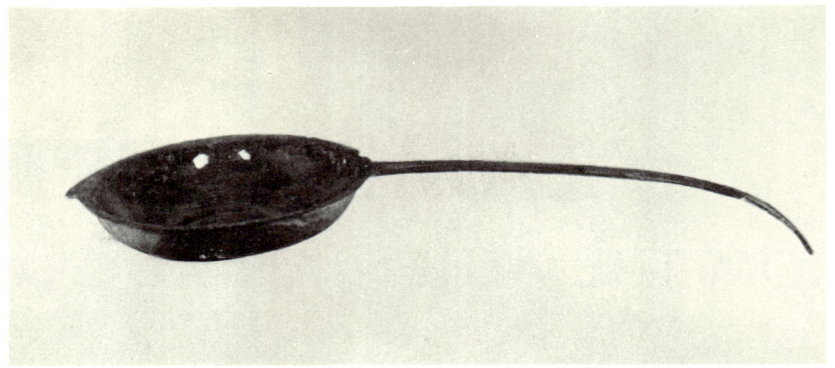

1. Copper Lamp from a Mycenaean Chamber Tomb, about 1450 B.C. B 704.

Pallas Athene went in front with a golden lamp, making a very fine light.
Homer, *Odyssey* XIX

Homer speaks of a lamp this once, when Odysseus and Telemachus working at night to remove the shields and spears out of their enemies' reach have their palace lit up by Athena, herself invisible.

After Mycenaean times the Athenians had no lamps until the early 7th century when the handmade lamp (2) appeared, an idea from the east. The development of the Attic clay lamp from this shape is illustrated on four pages at the end. The shape itself lived on in the east for millennia and reappeared in Attica in the 11th century A.D. (3).

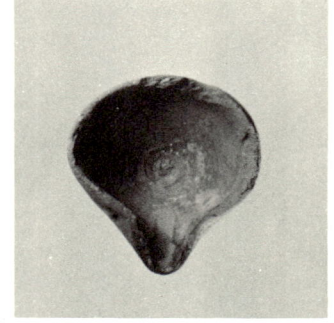

2. 7th century B.C. L 564.   3. 11th century A.D. L 1612.

FROM OPEN
TO CLOSED SHAPE

Simple functional objects reflect the characteristics of their time in an uncomplicated way. The 6th century lamp comes from an era of invention and experiment. The 5th century lamp is classical, providing a standard of lampmaking excellence with an outline defined by a single, wholly pleasing curve. The Hellenistic lamp, functionally more practical with its smaller opening and its hole on the side for the wick poker or for hanging, and artistically more elaborate, belongs to still another world.

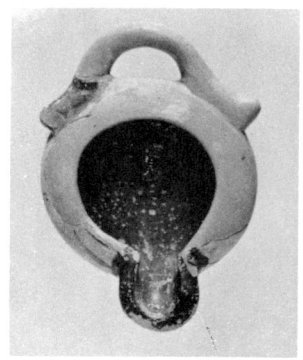

4. Archaic, Attic wheelmade
570–500 B.C. L 3806.

5. Classical, Attic wheelmade
465–425 B.C. L 4227.

6. Hellenistic, import, mouldmade
about 250 B.C. L 3779.

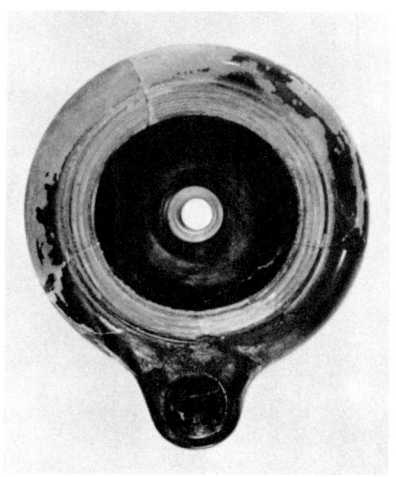

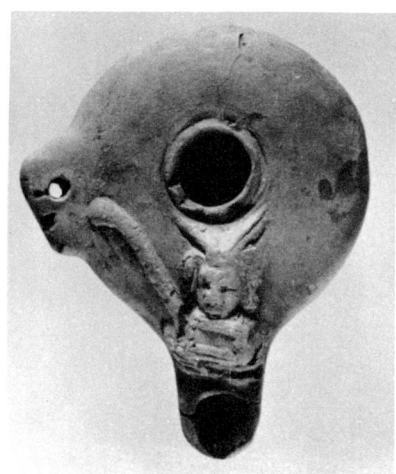

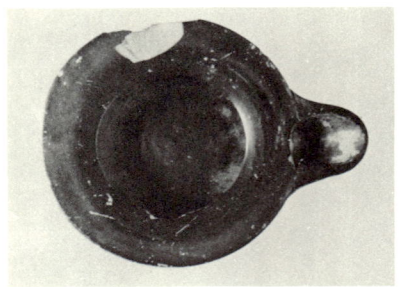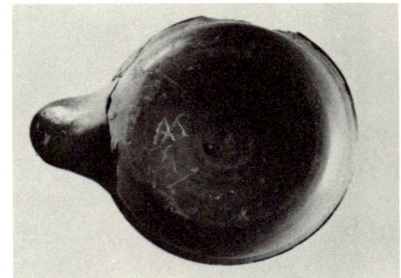

7. Lamp inscribed 'Ag,' Top and Bottom. L 2447.

AGASIKRATES AND HIS WELL

In 480/479 B.C. the Persians sacked Athens. After the victory of Salamis the Athenians recovered and cleaned up their town, throwing the debris into abandoned wells. One such well at the southwest corner of the Agora yielded household pottery, black-figured and red-figured pots, two loomweights, four bone styli for writing on waxed tablets (8), four lamps and a bronze arrowhead. A red-figured drinking cup, possibly by Euphronios, bore the love-name Agasikrates painted in purple (9). One of the lamps (7) has the letters alpha gamma scratched on the base, doubtless the beginning of the owner's name, Agasikrates. He also took care to scratch the same letters on the bases of two wine jugs (10, 11).

The rare name 'Agasikrates' occurs only once again, on a fragmentary inscription containing a list of names (12). The inscription was cut somewhat before the middle of the 5th century on a public funeral monument.

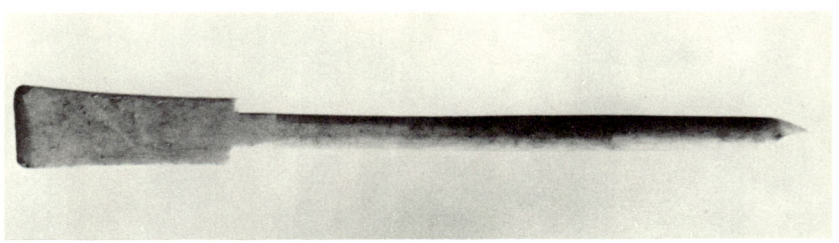

8. Bone stylus from Agasikrates' well. BI 292.

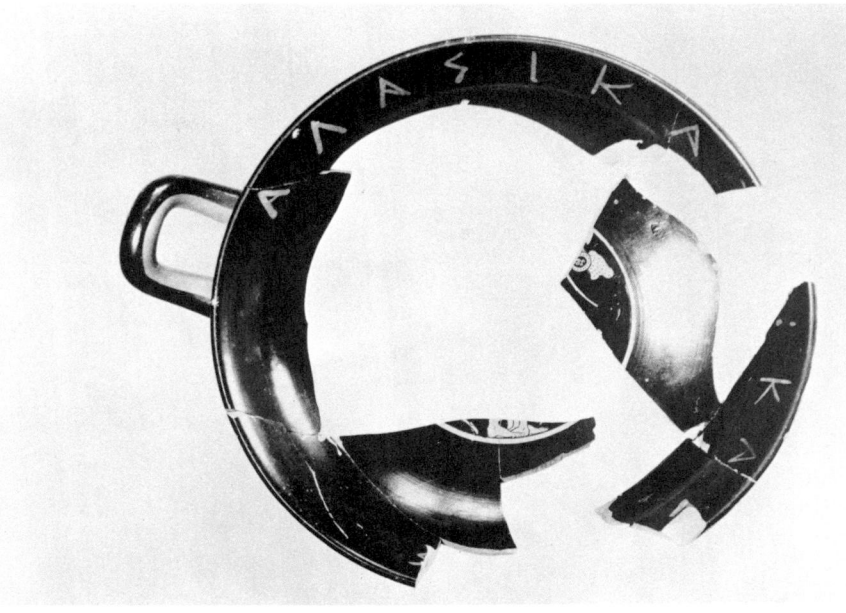

9. Cup with name of Agasikrates. P 7901.

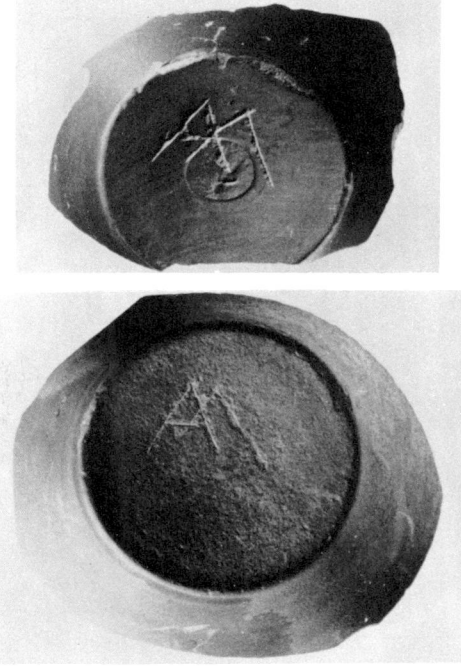

10, 11. Wine Jugs inscribed 'Ag.' P 8844, 8845.

12. Casualty List. I 953.

13. The floor of this 6th century lamp is drawn up into a central cone or *mesomphalos*. L 3445.

MICE AND LAMPS

In the mock epic *The Battle of Frogs and Mice* the mice used the *mesomphaloi* of lamps as shields.

After the mice had armed, Zeus called a council of the gods to determine which of the immortals would help the frogs and which would support the mice. When he asked Athena if she would go to the aid of the mice, she answered that she would never do that because the mice had done her much harm, ruining her lamps in their efforts to get at the oil.

Athena's unlucky enemies occasionally appear on lids provided to keep mice out of lamps.

14. Bronze Lamp Lid with Mouse. Roman period. Travlos collection.

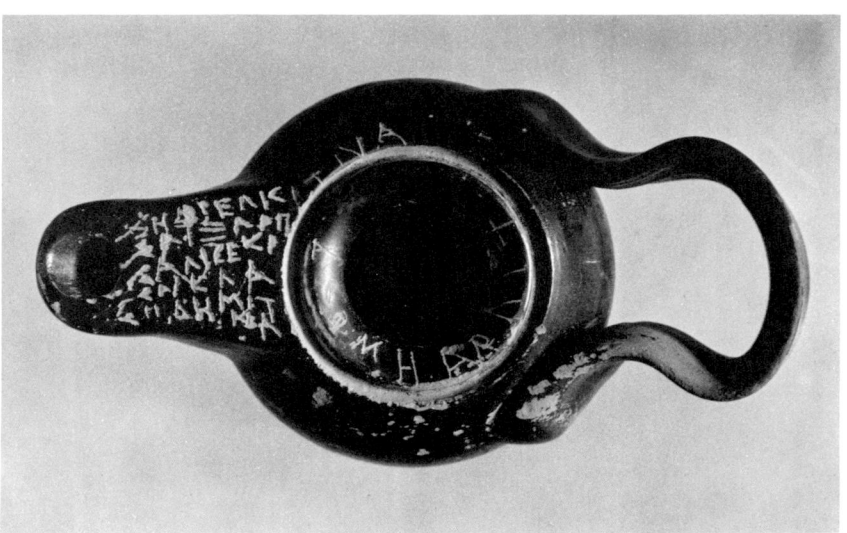

15. From beneath a house floor at the north foot of the Areopagus comes this perfectly preserved lamp of mid-4th century date. Six men's names appear scratched on top, all written in reverse: Philodemos, Antikleides, Praxias, Arkesilas, Alkias and Antimedes. Two trierarchs (rich men who fitted out warships) of 356/5 B.C. had the names Philodemos and Antikleides; a Praxias was overseer of the dockyards in 368/7 and an Arkesilas was guarantor for triremes (naval ships) in 340. Was this lamp perhaps a memento of some happy naval dinner party composed late in the proceedings? The backward writing, however, smacks of magic, and the lamp may have been deliberately buried under the floor as the bearer of a curse. L 5298.

16. Lamp of the late 3rd or 2nd century B.C., found not far from the site of the altar of Artemis Boulaia within the Tholos precinct. The inscription, divided between the two sides, reads 'sacred property of Artemis.' L 3918.

17. 3rd century B.C. L 2163.

Lamps with many nozzles lit up festive and ceremonial occasions. A nine-nozzle lamp (17) has a vertical tube in the center which could have been used in two ways. Either a stand with a tapering stick passing through the tube held the lamp aloft, or the lamp was suspended by a cord, knotted at the bottom of the tube to keep it in place. In Cleopatra's barge Antony especially admired the many lights which could be raised or lowered at will.

18. A lamp of the time of Socrates. Such a lamp burns from two to three hours, about the length of a dinner party, before it needs refilling, and it shines a little brighter than a candle. 425–400 B.C. L 4137.

19. Imported lamp in the shape of a bull's head, filleted for sacrifice, third quarter of the 2nd century B.C. The mouth is the wick-hole; when the flame was lit the animal would have reminded its owner of the fire-breathing bulls which Jason tamed on his quest for the golden fleece. L 3908.

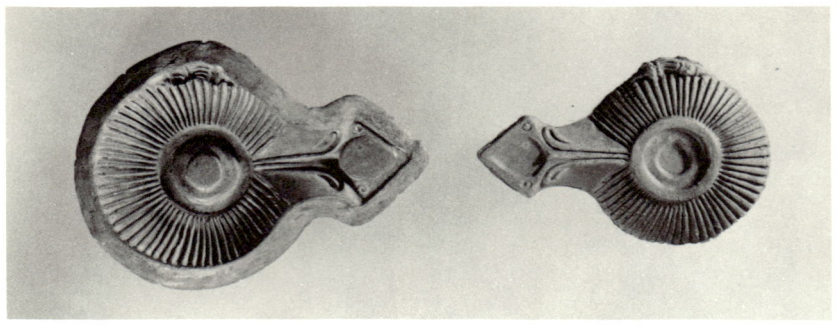

20. Ancient Mould for the Top of a Lamp and Modern Cast. L 3629.

LAMP MANUFACTURE IN ATHENS

Lamps were formed by hand from the early 7th to the early 5th century B.C. From around 650 B.C. to the 1st century A.D. lampmakers used the potter's wheel. Conservatism among the lampmakers appears in the way handmade lamps survived long after the wheelmade varieties had appeared, and, again, in the length of time it took the wheelmade lamps to lose the competition with the mouldmade process which was introduced in the beginning of the 3rd century B.C. and prevailed until the 8th century A.D. Moulds were the response to the demand for relief decoration on lamps. Like the potters, Attic lampmakers had at their disposal fine plastic clay (virtually begging to assume a shape) and the renowned black glaze which is made from clay. They readily found export markets all over Greece and the Aegean islands; many Attic lamps have been found in Egypt and South Russia.

21. The base of a mould-made lamp with the signature of Ariston who also signed other kinds of pottery. Late 2nd century B.C. L 1858.

IMPORTED LAMPS OF THE FIRST CENTURY A.D.

Turning from the export trade to imports, we find that only in the 1st and 2nd centuries A.D. did the Athenians import lamps in quantity, at first from Italy and Asia Minor, later from Corinth (see the following pages).

22. Imitation of a Bronze Lamp, from the Eastern Aegean area. L 2974.

23. Note the original wick made out of cloth. An olive spray, the source of the lamp fuel, enlivens the top, and in front is a ribbed jug, perhaps the filler from which the lamp was replenished with oil. L 4704.

24. Fragment of an Italian lamp disk with the head of a goddess in classicizing style, marred by the placing of the filling hole. L 4014.

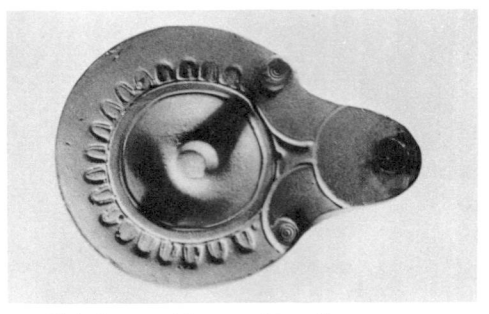

25. Plain lamp with central handle (the knob broken off). L 2843.

26. Rider. L 2415.

CORINTHIAN LAMPS OF THE SECOND CENTURY A.D.

27. Dionysiac reveller. L 5238.

28. Warrior holding shield; in field, corselet, crested helmet, greaves. L 595.

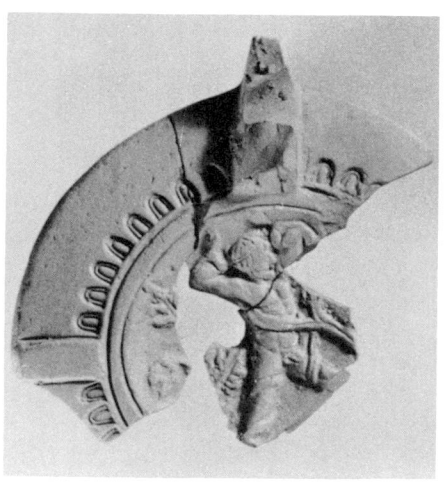

29. Lykourgos. L 3636.

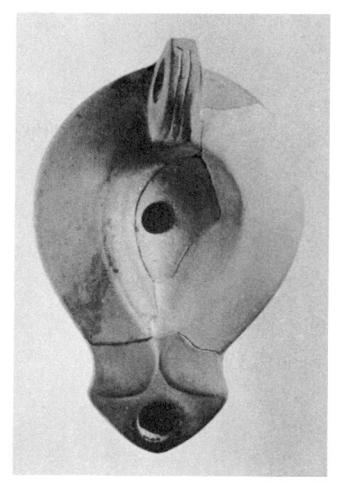

30. Plain lamp with semi-volutes. L 2996.

The *Dionysiaca* of Nonnus tells the myth of the Arabian king, Lykourgos, son of Ares, who, driven out of his mind by Hera, made war on her enemy Dionysos and his followers. When he attacked the nymph Ambrosia, she was by a miracle transformed into an embattled grape vine, winding around his body and throttling him. The rare relief on the lamp (29) gives the high point of the story when Lykourgos, far from giving up, defiantly shrieks for fire to burn up the vine Ambrosia.

31. Garden. L 1722.

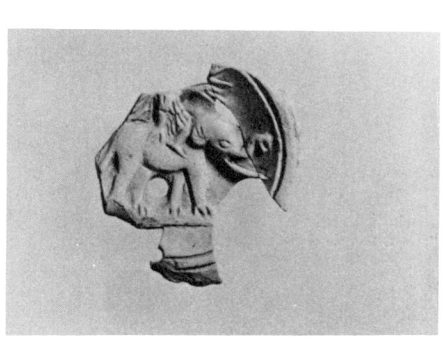

32. Mahout on elephant. L 3169.

33. Snarling leopardess; on base, signature of Sposianos. L 2413.

34. Hermes holding Caduceus, with his hand on the head of a prancing ram. The craftsmen in the great Athenian lampmaking establishments of the 3rd and 4th centuries A.D. often placed the owner's name or trademark on the underside of the lamp. Among the fifty known lampmaking shops that of Elpidephoros made the most graceful lamps and of all Elpidephoros' lamps this is the best. L 2810.

35. Worshipper bringing offerings on a tray to Aphrodite, whose statue stands in a small shrine with a domed roof. Attic lamp of the 3rd century A.D., signed by Preimos. L 2709.

36. Leda and the Swan. 3rd century A.D. L 519.

37. A night scene. Leander swims across the Hellespont to Hero who leans from a crenellated tower, guiding her lover with a lamp in her anxiously outstretched hand. 3rd century A.D. L 4251.

38. Athena, probably adapted from Pheidias' statue of Athena Promachos which stood on the Acropolis. 3rd century A.D. L 3731.

The goddess Athena and the hero Achilles protected Athens long after most other cities in the Roman Empire had embraced Christianity. In 396 A.D., we are told, a vision of Athena Promachos and Achilles above the Acropolis caused Alaric to withdraw his army of Goths without harming the city.

39. The Ransoming of Hector. Priam, kneeling, kisses the hand of Achilles who turns his head away. Hermes and the sorrowing Briseis stand behind. At the left is a mule drawing the cart with the ransom. Achilles' helmet lies beneath. 3rd century A.D. L 4490.

40–42. Lions of 3rd, 4th and 5th centuries. L 827, 1015, 4790.

LAMPS OF THE
THIRD, FOURTH AND FIFTH CENTURIES A.D.

The archetype, a solid lamp modelled in clay, is the start of each series of mouldmade lamps. The lampmaker drew pairs of upper and lower moulds from the archetype; from the moulds he cast lamps which he sold. When the moulds broke or wore out, the lampmaker often made new moulds from old lamps. Thus a representation was transferred from archetype to moulds to lamps (first generation), from lamps to moulds to lamps (second generation) and so on for three or four generations; such a series could run for as long as two centuries. The 4th century lion (41) and the 5th century lion (42) are direct or collateral descendants of the 3rd century lion (40); the same relationship holds true of the Poseidons (43–44), although it is hard to believe. The lions and the Poseidons show how the spirit and form of the representation were affected by the use of old blurred moulds and by the pointed graver of the retoucher whose criteria of art, as time passed, differed mightily from those of the artist of the archetype.

43, 44. Poseidon with dolphin and trident, 3rd and 4th centuries A.D. L 379, 571.

LAMPS IN THE FORM OF FIGURES OR OBJECTS

45. Dog. 3rd century A.D. L 2346.

46. Head of Silen. 1st century A.D. L 4966.

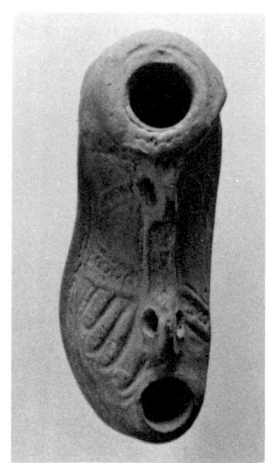
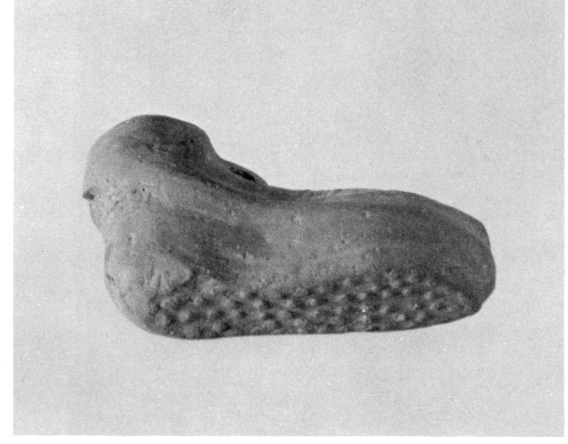

47. 'Thy Word is a lamp unto my feet and a light unto my path.' 6th century A.D. L 1881.

48. Panther drinking from wine jug. Panthers like wine because they are metamorphosed maenads. L 2294.

49. Bull, curled up. L 2710.

ANIMALS

The lamps on this and the facing page are Attic, 3rd–4th century A.D.

50. A cat or a weasel about to attack a cock who is pecking at a lizard. L 4462.

51. Athena's owl, fragment from the rim of a lamp. L 727.

52–53. Trainers feeding bear cubs. L 3862, 2569.

54. Acrobat somersaulting over bear. L 1092.

55. Bear fight in the arena. The man hangs on by his hands and feet to a sort of rack from which the bear attempts to dislodge him. L 2473.

56. Head of Dionysos' lion. L 5294.

57. Serapis and Isis in front of their temple. Serapis, enthroned, holds his scepter and touches Kerberos' head with his hand. Isis stands beside him holding a torch. 3rd century A.D. L 4274.

58. A unique lamp representing the *interpretatio graeca* of an Egyptian cult figure. The triple feather crown and mummy wrappings point to Isis. Mid-4th century A.D. L 3017.

Such lamps speak for the foreign cults flourishing in Athens until the end of the 4th century A.D.

59. 'Then Paul stood in the midst of Mars' hill and said, Ye men of Athens, I perceive that in all things ye are too superstitious.'
L 1153.

The 5th century lamp fragment with the head of Saint Paul (59) was found below the terrace which is on the upper north slope of the Areopagus where the church of St. Dionysios the Areopagite stood. Dionysios was a member of the Council of the Areopagus and St. Paul's first convert in Athens; he became the patron saint of Athens and his church was probably built on the spot where the Council of the Areopagus had met.

60. The Areopagus in the foreground, the Acropolis in the center and Mt. Hymettos in the background. The arrow points to the church of St. Dionysios.

61 62

CHRISTIAN AND JEWISH LAMPS

61. The earliest known Christian antiquity of Athens, a lamp with the cross monogram, chi rho, the initial letters of 'Christos.' Mid-4th century. L 762.

62. The earliest known Jewish antiquity of Athens, a lamp with the Menorah (seven-branched candlestick). Mid-4th century. L 2822.

63. Constantinian monogram with alpha and omega. Second half of 4th century. L 3208.

64. The Christian cross in this form is not known in Athens before the 5th century. Lamp signed by Soteria. Second quarter of 5th century. L 1062.

65. Christ with the cross. The angel hovering to the left of the cross and holding out a crown recalls Nike bearing the victor's wreath. Late 5th or 6th century. L 1275.

63 64 65

66. Fragment of a unique handle guard, showing Orpheus playing the lyre which rests on his knees (the upper part of the lyre is broken away). L 890.

67. Head of Fausta, wife of the Emperor Constantine. L 2354.

IMPORTED LAMPS, NORTH AFRICAN STYLE, FIFTH CENTURY A.D.

68. Round lamp, possibly from Sicily. L 754.

69. Late Hellenistic three-nozzle lamp. B 876.

BRONZE LAMPS

70. Christian lamp of the 5th century A.D. The filling hole has a lid in the form of a scallop shell which works on a hinge. On the nozzle and on the cross are rings to secure suspension chains. B 579.

71. Robust country godling, wrapped in hooded cloak. Such figures were meant to keep evil influences away. 3rd century A.D. B 455.

72. Handle guard in the form of an openwork palmette. A snake is coiled in the acanthus leaf at the center. 1st century A.D. B 433.

73. Krater-shaped candelabrum with inlaid laurel wreath. The well-wrought krater was made in the 1st century A.D.; the clumsy base is a repair of the 3rd century A.D. B 1182.

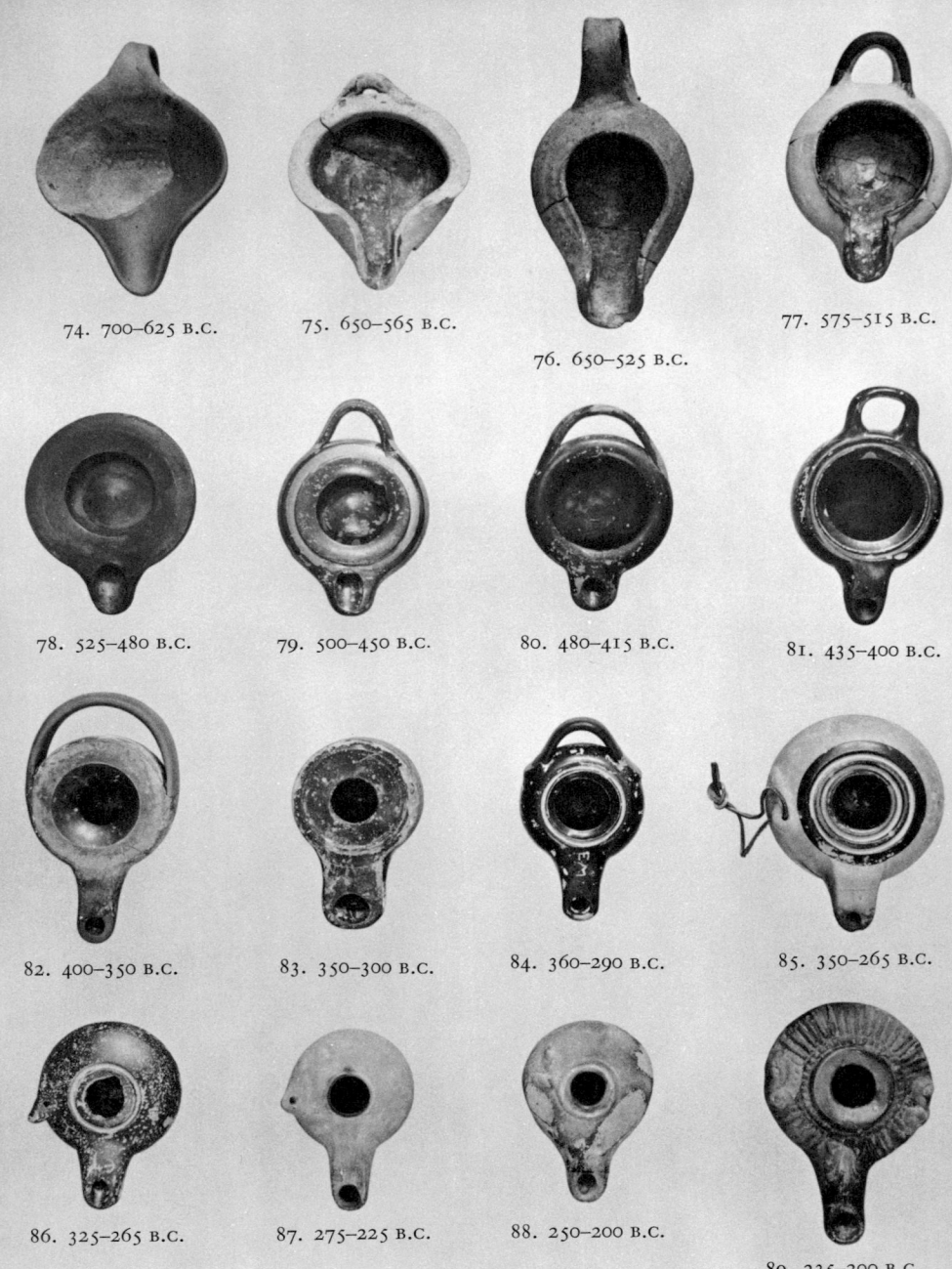

74. 700–625 B.C.   75. 650–565 B.C.   76. 650–525 B.C.   77. 575–515 B.C.

78. 525–480 B.C.   79. 500–450 B.C.   80. 480–415 B.C.   81. 435–400 B.C.

82. 400–350 B.C.   83. 350–300 B.C.   84. 360–290 B.C.   85. 350–265 B.C.

86. 325–265 B.C.   87. 275–225 B.C.   88. 250–200 B.C.   89. 235–200 B.C.

LAMP DEVELOPMENT 700–200 B.C.

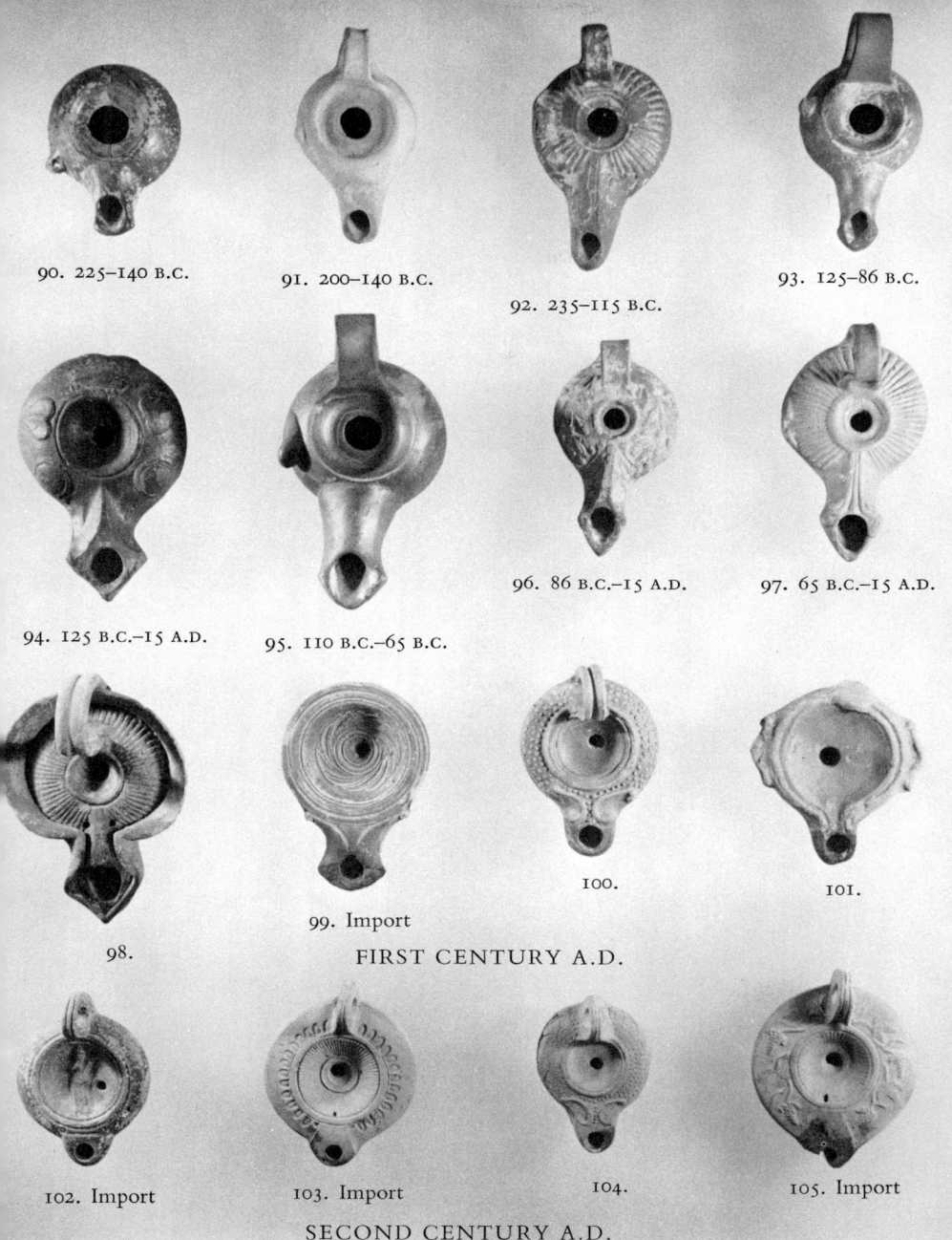

90. 225–140 B.C.   91. 200–140 B.C.   92. 235–115 B.C.   93. 125–86 B.C.

94. 125 B.C.–15 A.D.   95. 110 B.C.–65 B.C.   96. 86 B.C.–15 A.D.   97. 65 B.C.–15 A.D.

98.   99. Import   100.   101.

FIRST CENTURY A.D.

102. Import   103. Import   104.   105. Import

SECOND CENTURY A.D.

LAMP DEVELOPMENT 200 B.C. – 200 A.D.

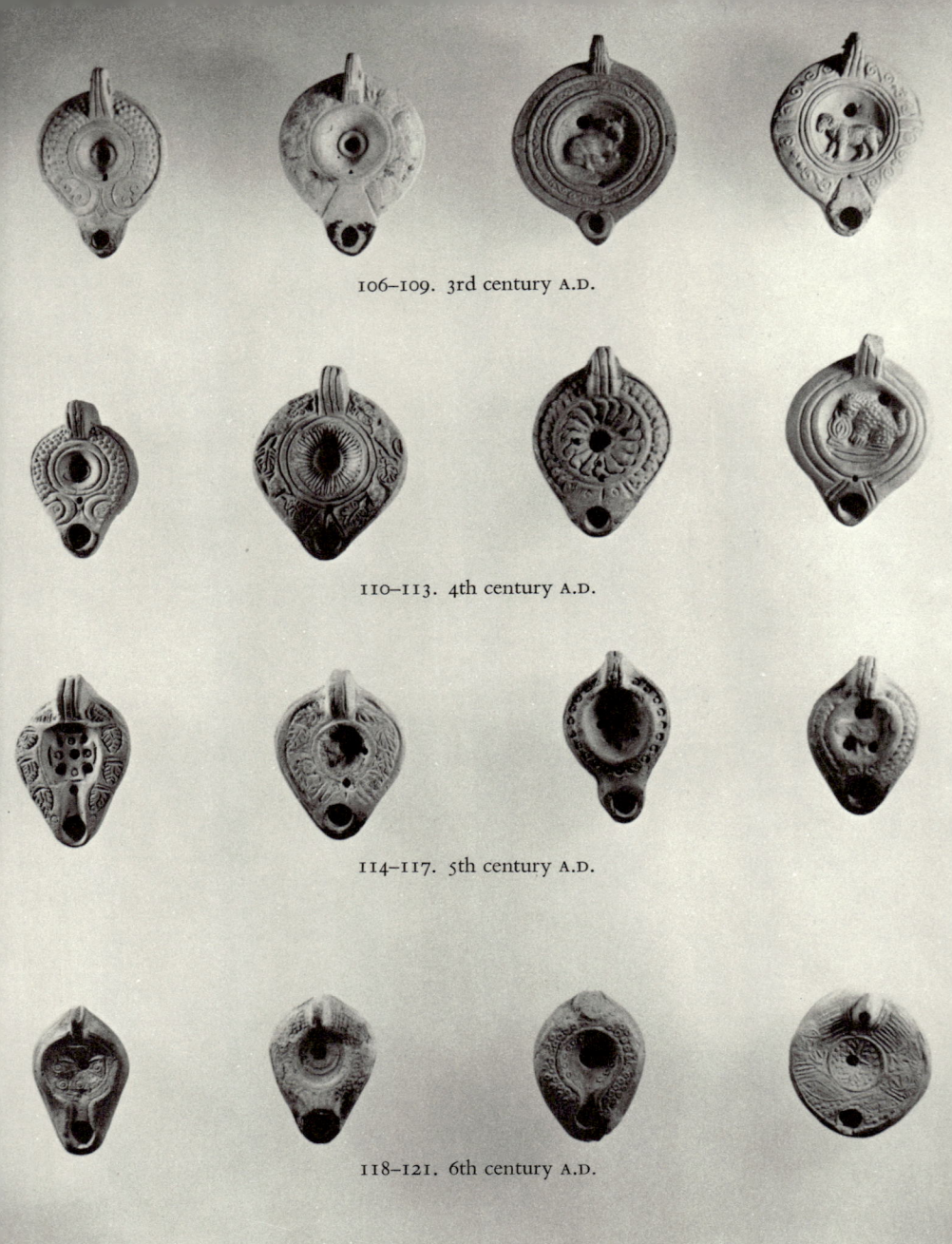

106–109. 3rd century A.D.

110–113. 4th century A.D.

114–117. 5th century A.D.

118–121. 6th century A.D.

LAMP DEVELOPMENT 200–700 A.D.

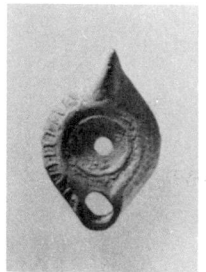  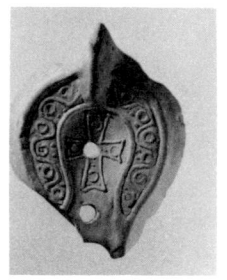 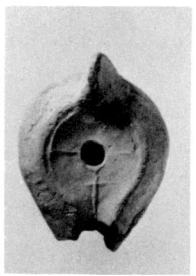

122–125. 7th century A.D.

Lamps and letters came and went together. The arrival of the clay lamp in Attica coincides with the appearance of the alphabet on inscribed sherds from Mount Hymettos in the early 7th century B.C. In the 7th century A.D. literature and lamps alike were extinguished. No lamps in the Agora have as yet been identified as belonging to the 8th–9th centuries A.D., the Dark Ages.

NOTE ON NOS. 74–127

The dates given are approximations; the reader should understand a *circa* before each date where a year is mentioned. The scale is about one-fourth natural size. Nos. 74 and 76 are handmade lamps; Nos. 75, 77–87, 90, 93, 95 and 126 are wheelmade; the other lamps are mouldmade.

126. Byzantine Period. L 1680.   127. Turkish Period. LB 1247.

128. Hephaistos, the smith-god who made Zeus' throne and Achilles' armor, is shown holding in his left hand a torch and in his right a hammer (partly visible). The lamp relief of the 3rd century A.D. may be an echo of the lost cult statue of Hephaistos which stood together with a statue of Athena in the Temple of Hephaistos overlooking the Athenian Agora. L 5413.

Most of the lamps illustrated in this booklet have been published in the
following volumes of *The Athenian Agora, Results of Excavations conducted by
the American School of Classical Studies at Athens*, Princeton, New Jersey:
IV: *Greek Lamps and their Survivals* by R. H. Howland, 1958
VI: *Terracottas and Plastic Lamps of the Roman Period* by C. Grandjouan, 1961
VII: *Lamps of the Roman Period* by J. Perlzweig, 1961
No. 14 is published by the kind permission of the J. Travlos family.

INVENTORY NUMBERS

74. L 3022	82. L 4024	91. L 3801	100. L 2907	109. L 3508	118. L 2341
75. L 5362	83. L 1521	92. L 553	101. L 1382	110. L 983	119. L 2875
76. L 4146	84. L 4212	93. L 1306	102. L 3329	111. L 2442	120. L 1889
77. L 2678	85. L 4021	94. L 3091	103. L 3008	112. L 4281	121. L 1052
78. L 5157	86. L 2360	95. L 4358	104. L 4925	113. L 2294	122. L 3484
79. L 5328	87. L 3524	96. L 4487	105. L 2411	114. L 1063	123. L 3810
80. L 2322	88. L 3777	97. L 4705	106. L 5087	115. L 22	124. L 3802
81. L 3804	89. L 1846	98. L 1840	107. L 2300	116. L 819	125. L 3758
	90. L 461	99. L 3358	108. L 2710	117. L 5223	

EXCAVATIONS OF THE ATHENIAN AGORA
PICTURE BOOKS

1. *Pots and Pans of Classical Athens* (1951)
2. *The Stoa of Attalos II in Athens* (1959)
3. *Miniature Sculpture from the Athenian Agora* (1959)
4. *The Athenian Citizen* (1960)
5. *Ancient Portraits from the Athenian Agora* (1960)
6. *Amphoras and the Ancient Wine Trade* (1961)
7. *The Middle Ages in the Athenian Agora* (1961)
8. *Garden Lore of Ancient Athens* (1963)
9. *Lamps from the Athenian Agora* (1964)
10. *Inscriptions from the Athenian Agora* (1966)
11. *Waterworks in the Athenian Agora* (1968)
12. *An Ancient Shopping Center: The Athenian Agora* (1971)
13. *Early Burials from the Agora Cemeteries* (1973)
14. *Graffiti in the Athenian Agora* (1974)
15. *Greek and Roman Coins in the Athenian Agora* (1975)
16. *The Athenian Agora: A Short Guide* (1976)
    German and French editions (1977)
17. *Socrates in the Agora* (1978)
18. *Mediaeval and Modern Coins in the Athenian Agora* (1978)

These booklets are obtainable from the
American School of Classical Studies at Athens
c/o Institute for Advanced Study, Princeton, N.J. 08540, U.S.A.
Price: $1.00 except No. 8, $1.50
They are also available in the Agora Museum, Stoa of Attalos, Athens